The Prodigal Mother

JUDY WILLS LOWDER

With Creative Contributions from Sarah Lowder

The Prodigal Mother
Judy Wills Lowder

ISBN-13: 978-1974060887
ISBN-10: 1974060888

Available from Amazon.com and other retail outlets

New International Version®, NIV® Copyright © 2011 by Biblica, Inc.® Used by permission. All rights reserved worldwide. New King James Version®. Copyright© 1982 by Thomas Nelson, Inc. Used by permission. All rights reserved. New American Standard, NAS: Scripture taken from the New American Standard Bible®, copyright© 1960, 1962, 1963, 1968, 1971, 1972, 1973, 1975, 1977, 1995 by The Lockman Foundation. Used by permission. King James Version, KJV: King James Version, public domain. New Living Translation, Copyright© 1996, 2004, 2007 by Tyndale House Foundation. Used by permission of Tyndale House Publishers, Inc., Carol Stream, Illinois 60188. All rights reserved. Used by permission. King James 2000 Copyright© 2001 by Robert A. Couric. Used with permission.

Scriptures in this book are from the New International Version unless otherwise specified.

If you would like to order books from the author or do any of the above, you may contact Olivet Counseling Services at:

judywillslowder@swissmail.org

TABLE OF CONTENTS

Dedication

This book is dedicated to my prodigal parents, Paul and Hilda Wills. Dad gave me a life-long love for learning and Mother instilled I could accomplish anything if I tried really hard. After years of prodigal living I came to my senses. Later, when I apologized and asked your forgiveness, you responded with quizzical looks; it was as though you could not remember. This response was quite like our Father who remembers our sins no more.

What a tremendous blessing to work in the editing process with my talented daughter. Sarah's creative input in developing Shabar's story was invaluable and I deeply appreciate the support and patience of my husband, Steve.

The Prodigal Mother originated with and was breathed upon by the Holy Spirit.

The Parable of the Lost Son

JESUS CONTINUED: "There was a man who had two sons. The younger one said to his father, 'Father, give me my share of the estate.' So he divided his property between them.

"Not long after that, the younger son got together all he had, set off for a distant country and there squandered his wealth in wild living. After he had spent everything, there was a severe famine in that whole country, and he began to be in need. So he went and hired himself out to a citizen of that country, who sent him to his fields to feed pigs. He longed to fill his stomach with the pods that the pigs were eating, but no one gave him anything.

"When he came to his senses, he said, 'How many of my father's hired servants have food to spare, and here I am starving to death! I will set out and go back to my father and say to him: Father, I have sinned against heaven and against you. I am no longer worthy to be called your son; make me like one of your hired servants. So he got up and went to his father.

"But while he was still a long way off, his father saw him and was filled with compassion for him; he ran to his son, threw his arms around him and kissed him.

"The son said to him, 'Father, I have sinned against heaven and against you. I am no longer worthy to be called your son.'

"But the father said to his servants, 'Quick! Bring the best robe and put it on him. Put a ring on his finger and sandals on his feet. Bring the fattened calf and kill it. Let's have a feast and celebrate. For this son of mine was dead and is alive again; he was lost and is found.' So they began to celebrate.

"Meanwhile, the older son was in the field. When he came near the house, he heard music and dancing. So he called one of the servants and asked him what was going on. 'Your brother has come,' he replied, 'and your father has killed the fattened calf because he has him back safe and sound.'

"The older brother became angry and refused to go in. So his father went out and pleaded with him. But he answered his father, "Look! All these years I've been slaving for you and never disobeyed your orders. Yet you never gave me even a young goat so I could celebrate with my friends. But when this son of yours who has squandered your property with prostitutes comes home, you kill the fattened calf for him!'

"My son,' the father said, 'you are always with me, and everything I have is yours. But we had to celebrate and be glad, because this brother of yours was dead and is alive again; he was lost and is found."

Luke 15:11-32 New International Version (NIV)

Definitions

Prodigal:
> "A person who spends money or resources freely and recklessly; wastefully extravagant."
Merriam Webster

Prodigal Son
> "A man or boy who has left his family to do something that the family disapproves of and has now returned home feeling sorry for what he has done."
Cambridge Dictionary

For the purposes of this fiction, a Prodigal son or daughter is one who participates in a lifestyle divergent from the family's beliefs or values. A Prodigal Mother is one who loves such a child.

Many phrases in this text, which you may google, are paraphrased Bible verses.

Characters

Shabar: The Prodigal Mother. Her name means to be broken and crushed

Saul: Shabar's husband

Hildah: Her character counsels Shabar and epitomizes the role of the Holy Spirit

Rabbi Hokhmah: His name means wisdom and his character personifies Father God

Chazaq: The older son. His name means strong

Chen: The Prodigal Son. His name means grace

Jacob: Hildah's son

Shabar's story is not a historically correct theological discourse. It is a fictional story delivered to the Body of Christ to teach and encourage.

My Story

You don't know me. You probably never even thought about me, but my complex family situation is well known to generations of believers. Since Jesus taught in Galilee, countless sermons have been based on the stories of my husband, my older son and my younger son through the Parable of the Prodigal Son. I am the Prodigal Mother.

Providing encouragement to future generations of women is my intention. Despite being behind the scenes, you will understand the significant role I played and why the story needs to be told. I want to share what I learned. Following are excerpts from my diary; sometimes redundant and often rambling, which I transposed into this narrative. When possible, I attempted to use your contemporary vernacular. Hopefully my experience will encourage and comfort those who walk a similar path.

It began while my husband was on a business trip. My oldest son, Chazaq, came by to check on me one morning and said, "after all you and Father have done for us, I cannot believe Chen asked for his inheritance and left the family."

What was he saying? My mind could not process what my ears heard. It felt like a huge boulder rolled into my heart as I fell to the ground.

"Mother," he said, "I am so sorry. I thought you knew. Did Father not tell you last week?"

"Chen left us?" I asked. Feeling dazed, was I hearing correctly? My mind fought to comprehend.

"Yes, Mother. It is despicable! Chen should have told you himself…I thought you knew. I begged him to at least bid you farewell, but he swore angry, shameful utterances which I shall not repeat. It was shocking. Father told me he would tell you before he left… I regret to inform you of this traitorous act. Needless to say, Chen is no longer my brother. Jacob is my only brother."

"Oh, Jehovah Ezer, My Helper," were the only words I could whisper as blood pumped quickly and heavily throughout my body. The sound of Chazaq's voice echoed, but the words remained unprocessed.

"Mother, are you sure you are alright?" he asked as he helped me sit in a chair. He poured a cup of water and I assured him, "I'm fine."

"I would stay here with you, but Jacob and I are to meet the men in the city this morning. Shall I get Aunt Hildah?"

"Yes, Chazaq, go to your meeting. No, please don't call Hildah, I need a moment to myself. I am okay."

"Mother, again, I am so sorry to tell you of this disgrace. I do not know why Father delayed this announcement," he said as he headed out.

It was good to be alone. Numbness yielded to an avalanche of emotions tumbling through my mind and heart. I did not know which to feel first. Eventually, dizziness abated and my equilibrium momentarily steadied. How long I sat in the chair, I do not know.

Hearing Hildah on the portico, I hastened upstairs. I was desperate to confide in her but possessed no articulate thoughts or words. My thoughts resonated. Sprinting throughout my mind; propelling me faster and faster up the stairs. Upon entering my chamber, I collapsed on the bed. It cannot be true that my son is gone. It cannot be true. Why would Chen leave our family?

As I cried out to Yahweh, I asked, "what have we done?" It is written to have one's children taken away is a curse. Yahweh, my LORD, "what have we done?" Our child was taken away … by what? He wanted to leave. He was carried away by his own lusts. He wanted to leave. He wanted to leave our family and our LORD, which was much worse than having a son taken away.

Feeling rejected and cast aside, I humbly inquired, "My LORD, we labor to keep the Law and Saul faithfully presents tithes and offerings. He offers sacrifices and we observe the feasts. We keep the Shabbat and never miss synagogue. My LORD, my LORD, what have we done to bring this upon ourselves? Are we punished for a sin?"

My thoughts returned to Saul. When we married, he was a widow with three young children. The little boy and two tiny daughters were the joy of my life. Their mother passed away before they were old enough to remember. We honored her memory and often spoke of her; but Saul's children knew and loved me as their mother. Years later when The LORD answered our prayers for a son, they rejoiced at Chen's birth and adored their baby brother. Chazaq mentored and the girls doted on their little sibling. He was light hearted and added joy to our family. We carefully taught the Law to our children and they did not depart from the teachings.

The brothers were opposites. Chazaq was reserved and serious, while Chen was outgoing and playful. We sometimes noticed Chen did not diligently study the Torah and the writings. This I attributed to his independent nature for he was not an evil young man. In honest retrospect, Chen was increasingly disinterested in synagogue and neglectful of the Tanakh. He disengaged from us during recent Shabbat dinners. Why didn't I see the warning signs? Still, it was unthinkable for him to leave our family, our people and our LORD. Maybe he will change his mind and return home.

Saul! He did not tell me. Never had I experienced such anger and hurt towards him. He knew Chen was leaving and did not tell me. How could he keep this from me? I had every right to know our son planned to leave for a far country. Surely it took several days to get the inheritance arranged. Saul knew and kept this tragedy from me.

As my anger escalated to rage, I was glad he was away in Tiberius for a long business trip. Why didn't Saul refuse Chen's request? Why didn't Saul tell him, "this is ridiculous!" Chen would have moved past the wanderlust in a couple of weeks. Instead, Saul complied and left on a business trip without telling me.

Chen and I were always close. He was such an easy child to love. Saul's mother criticized my parenting skills.

She said I spoiled Chen as a toddler, but I admired his determination and strong will. Had Saul informed me of Chen's intentions, perhaps I could have reasoned with him and dissuaded. Instead my son was gone.

Memories of my mother-in-law's chastisement perforated my soul like fiery spears. She negatively compared my mothering to Saul's first wife and what hurt the most was that she was right. Her children were exemplary and the one I bore left our family, our people and our LORD.

The dull fury towards Saul rolled to Chen. How could my son leave without a farewell? He vanished! I did not understand. I could not understand. I would never understand how my son left without a farewell. I would never understand why my husband did not tell me. There was a sorrowful expression in Saul's eyes last week, but I reasoned he was tired. Why didn't he tell me? I would have chased after Chen had I known the direction in which he travelled.

Thoughts and emotions circulated with devastating fear and condemnation. I wanted to speak with Hildah, but trying to form a coherent thought or sentence was futile. Besides, it was late and she was sleeping.

Heartache wrenched my thoughts and took captive my spirit. Wrestling the darkness proved useless; I was left devoid of sleep. Misery was an unwelcome yet constant partner during the daylight hours which refused to cease. They merely crawled, spreading into a dismal twilight. As another moon rose, cloaking all beneath its silvery drape, I remained imprisoned; sentenced to another abysmal night. Over and over I implored answers of The LORD. I called out to Him in my time of distress because I needed His strength to take my next breath. Of course I did not expect The LORD to respond to this disgraceful situation. Hoping to find answers from within, the pleading questions were rhetorical.

What did I do wrong as a Mother? Perhaps I should have heeded my mother-in-law's advice to turn his raising over to Hildah. I did not intend to spoil Chen as Saul's mother alleged, I just loved him so much. Not once did Hildah suggest he was spoiled. We never held back our opinions and she would have told me if I was spoiling Chen. What did our family do to bring on this disgrace - a child turning from his LORD and family? What did we do wrong? Again and again, the persistent questions yielded heaping self-recrimination, but remained unanswered.

Hildah overheard the wailing. She gently approached me in tears, asking if there was anything she could do to help. I found her concern comforting as she wept with me. Hildah drew alongside me the way she had done throughout our lives. A comforter in times of strife. A helper in times of chaos. Even when I desired solitude, knowing her presence dwelt within the house provided reassurance.

Our mothers were cousins. A year older than I,

Hildah was orphaned at age four. Hildah's uncle, Rabbi Hokhmah, who was unmarried at the time, chose my parents to raise her. I could not remember life without Hildah who knew everything about me. In fact, Hildah seemed to know me better than I knew myself. I however, could never understand her. It is essential to describe Hildah because she is a pillar of my story. She led when I did not think I could continue. My teacher and advisor, she counseled with truth and gently confronted when needed. Hildah was always tender, never judgmental. Many regarded her life as characterized by tragedy; losing her parents at a young age and widowed with a newborn son. Instead, as a close observer, I saw a life marked by joy and gratitude.

We were blessed because we were taught to read and write. Our parents required our brothers to teach us what they were taught in synagogue each day. I knew as much about the Scriptures and The LORD as Hildah, but she had a level of understanding and discernment that I lacked.

Hildah, newly widowed with an infant son, Jacob, dismissed marriage proposals and agreed to supervise my household when I married Saul. We actually wanted my sister to live with us because she was a refreshing person, but she insisted upon a duty. She and her baby were a blessing to us. Jacob grew up with our children who regarded him as a brother. Saul fondly claimed Hildah as the sister he never had and raised her baby as a son.

Saul frequently described me as a wife of great value, more precious than jewels. He told me, "I have found a good thing and my heart trusts in you."

Early on I said to him, "you know the key to success in our household is Hildah. She makes me look like the virtuous woman and never accepts any credit."

"My darling, you had the brilliance to bring her into our home," he chuckled. Saul's kindness was inconsistent with the dismissive manner in which he treated me when Chen left.

To Hildah I cried furiously and reiterated my questions. Never have I acted so hysterically, but I could be myself with her. Hildah speculated it was too painful for Chen to bid farewell and too difficult for Saul to inform. She listened, empathized and simultaneously shared my hurt.

"Did you already know?" I asked.

"Of course not," she replied. "Chazaq kept coming by to check on you. He told me this morning when I asked what was going on. Had I known, Chen would never have left...we would have stopped him."

Considering Hildah's losses, I cautioned not to wallow in self-pity, but she told me, "my dear Shabar, it is good to cry out to The LORD."

"It is?"

"Remember? The Prophet Jeremiah instructs us to 'pour out our hearts like water in the presence of The LORD' and King David wrote 'pour out your hearts to him'," she said.

"But that was ages ago and it was regarding our people in times of distress," I argued.

"It is in the Tanakh! Yes, it is historical, but it is for us today. I believe everything written about Israel and our people applies to us personally," she stated.

"Come now Hildah, we must not misconstrue the Scriptures to accommodate ourselves."

"The prophet Jeremiah wrote, 'Is not MY word like fire,' declares The LORD, 'and like a hammer that breaks a rock in pieces?'. Seems rather direct and powerful to me."

"Besides," she answered, "The LORD told me."

Was Hildah not the wisest, most righteous woman I knew, I would have warned of blasphemy. Rabbi Hokhmah, her uncle, granted access to the Torah scroll and writings and she had memorized much Scripture.

"How do you say The LORD told you?"

"He has spoken to me always," came the reply.

"Your entire life? When was the first time?"

"When I was five. When I first understood my parents had passed on and I was an orphan."

"Where were you and what did The LORD say? Help me understand how He speaks to you."

"We were at the synagogue on Shabbat. The reading was from the Prophet Isaiah, 'I have accepted you and not rejected you.' Rejection came upon me when I realized I did not have a Father or Mother like most children," she explained. "Your parents were truly my parents in every sense. They treated me equally, often favored me as a daughter, but there was a lingering, internalized orphan spirit. I entered the synagogue that day as an orphan and left with a Father. Shabar, sometimes it seems you have an orphan spirit because you do not understand how much The LORD loves you."

"Of course Papa has passed on, but I am a grown woman, not a child."

"Our age does not matter if we do not know how much The LORD loves us. Shabar, don't you realize we truly belong to Him? It is not a criticism."

"Do you hear him audibly?"

"No, it's a still, quiet voice. I told Papa 'The LORD

told me he was my Father and now I have two.' He gathered me to his lap and said, 'Indeed you do Hildah. You have The LORD and you have me'. Papa believed me."

"Hildah, let us not engage in your orphan spirit philosophy at this time. Perhaps Papa was humoring you. I want to know more about The LORD speaking to you. The example to which you referred was the Rabbi reading the Scripture. That is not The LORD speaking to you. This makes no sense. You said The LORD speaks. How do you know it is The LORD speaking?"

"Because He always speaks what is written in the Scriptures, usually from the writings or the prophets. I typically go to my uncle, tell him what The LORD spoke and he shows me where it is written in the scrolls or writings. That is how I know The LORD is speaking. He speaks His Word. The LORD spoke directly to Moses. The prophets were inspired by The LORD, usually in visions or dreams. The LORD speaks His Word to me. He frequently recalls His Word to me."

"Besides the synagogue, where are you when He speaks to you? I really want to know."

"The LORD also speaks to me in the *Secret Place*, within His shelter."

"King David likely composed that writing in his palace."

"It is written, 'He who dwells in the *Secret Place* of the Most High', not just King David".

"Well, 'he' means 'man'. Does that apply to women?"

"Remember, 'he' sometimes means men or women, humans. Anyway, we are His daughters. If you read the parchments closely you will understand and this is what Rabbi Hokhmah teaches."

I greatly regretted my inattentiveness to Scripture and detailed teaching, "So that is why you never seemed distraught about not having a Mother or Father...or losing your husband?"

"Yes and one day, in my *Secret Place*, the Spirit of The LORD resounded 'He is a father to the fatherless and a husband to the widow'. He told me my baby and I were carved in the palm of his hand. I never worried about Jacob's welfare again."

"Hildah, I'm going to try to be strong like you."

She laughed, "no, never try to be strong."

"If you are not strong, how have you survived?"

"Hosea wrote, 'you have eaten the fruit of deception because you depended on your own strength'. Similarly, Joel wrote, 'let the weakling say I am strong'. The LORD imparts His strength through the Scripture. 'The joy of

The LORD is my strength' is not a platitude. It is my reality as much as you and I having this conversation."

I always perceived Hildah as a bit of a *Pollyannah*. However, this was the key to her joy and overcoming adversity in her life! She did not attempt to cope with life in her own strength, but relied on the strength of The LORD. It was counterintuitive and I was uncertain if I could ever attain this perspective.

Knowing this was not foolishness, I so desired to be like Hildah. Momentarily, I forgot my son left our family and our LORD. Conversations with Hildah always provided a reprieve.

Saul soon returned. We embraced and wept when he entered my chamber. This was the only time in our marriage when I witnessed Saul crying. Strong and dignified, he was a noble man, respected by the men at the gate. "I am sorry. I could not summon the words to tell you before I left," he said. Hildah was right. My husband did not tell me because it was too painful. "We must continue on with our lives," he said with sad resignation.

As usual we went to synagogue on the Shabbat, an activity I secretly and silently loathed after Chen's departure. Perceived by many women as haughty, I knew most accepted me because of my husband's status and my relationship with Hildah, who was loved by all. She understood my aloof facade compensated for feelings of inadequacy and insecurity. Introverted, I was awkwardly uncomfortable with superficial chit chat and pleasantries.

Two genuine friends offered heartfelt comfort. The other old biddies knew about Chen and I surmised a couple were gleeful over my loss. Several offered condolences and suggested he was dead to us and no longer existed. Their remarks, I supposed, were intended to make me feel better. Hildah overheard the comments and kept quiet.

Chen was circumcised, dedicated and taught like the others. Each Shabbat sparked a grief reaction. Chazaq, Jacob and the other fine young men at the synagogue continually reflected back my failure. If I did not raise my child well, then my entire life was wasted. If I failed as a Mother, I failed at life itself. These tumultuous thoughts and emotions spawned inner shrieks, which echoed Job's lament for a mediator between himself and The LORD; only He could help me and my family.

My emotions of failure, betrayal, condemnation and bitterness were too embarrassing to share. I detested many people as intensely as I loathed myself. It was only to The LORD, quite tentatively at first, and myself that I expressed my tightly concealed, noxious feelings. He did not strike me dead, proving truth in the Scriptures. His mercies were new every morning. Despite the cognitive dissonance, His Word was gradually becoming more personal.

Judy Wills Lowder

Life continued without Chen although it was hugely barren for me. My life was devoted to loving my husband and raising our children. Chen was gone and my husband was sorrowfully silent. My life's work had been in vain. It was nothing.

"My family is in ruins," I cried to Hildah.

Quoting the prophet Isaiah, she said, "Surely The LORD will look with compassion on all your ruins."

We continued our debate about the Scripture applying to our lives personally or to Israel. When I admitted I felt rejected by Chen, Hildah's quote from Isaiah, "I have accepted you and not rejected you," provided comfort. Was this how Scripture applied to my life?

Once I exclaimed to Hildah, "I'm so ashamed. I'm ashamed of my son. The disgrace I feel is tangible when we go to the city or to the synagogue. It chases me. I'm ashamed of myself."

Hildah again responded with a quote from the prophet Isaiah, "instead of your shame you will receive a double portion, and instead of disgrace you will rejoice in your inheritance."

"What meaning does that have for my life, Hildah?"

"It means what it says."

"But what does it mean for my shame and disgrace?"

"It means what it says," Hildah responded. Hildah knew the entire parchment from the prophet Isaiah by memory. Cautiously, I began to comprehend the personal application and loved to hear her cite passages as she went about her day.

Another day, she quoted, "I will contend with those who contend with you, and your children I will save. More than once," she continued, "Moses said The LORD will fight for you."

Reverting to doubt, I inquired, "how do you randomly reference these Scriptures?"

"I do not know. You are going through a battle and The LORD brings Scripture to my mind."

"The LORD brings thoughts to your mind? Hildah, I don't want to be contentious, but you continue to baffle. I have never heard anything like this."

"Yes you have. The LORD provided Nehemiah with fantastic thoughts and ideas."

"Nehemiah? He did a great work for The LORD to rebuild the wall around Jerusalem. Do you think we have the same status as he?"

"Yes, 'we are His people, the sheep of His pasture'.

Judy Wills Lowder

The same as Nehemiah and Moses."

"Back to my shame and disgrace. What does it mean that The LORD will have compassion on all my ruins? Hildah, what does it mean The LORD will contend for me?"

"You must ask The LORD what this means for your life," she said. "Shabar, I see your pain and despair. You are up and down, dependent upon and being controlled by your emotions instead of focusing on the truth. I am asking Elohim to hover over yourself and Chen, just as he hovered over the waters back in the beginning. The LORD will give you revelation and insight from the Torah and the writings."

This seemed brazen to me, but when Hildah spoke it seemed so normal. Added to my shame and disgrace was self-condemnation for my inability to make applicable the teachings from the Tanakh like Hildah. If only I had persistently studied and pursued The LORD when everything in my life was wonderful, I thought regretfully, perhaps I would have more wisdom and revelation for this crisis.

It was while Hildah visited friends in Tabgha that I really floundered. The truth from the Torah and the writings were mitigated as my thoughts ruminated on the circumstance. The distress overwhelmed to the point I considered fleeing to another village where no one knew my story. I was too old for employment as a servant so the idea was not feasible. Besides, it wasn't fair to Saul and the other children and grandchildren who did nothing but love and affirm.

My husband continued to treat me kindly and never shared his hurt or grief. Saul tenderly hugged and reiterated how much the other children loved me. Children I did not bear loved me, and I them; but it did not alleviate the painful rejection of the child I bore. I refrained from crying around Saul because my tears fomented a mournful expression on his characteristically pleasant face. He wanted me to be happy.

In addition to hurt and rejection, I was anguished by the appalling character of the child I birthed and raised. The responsibility for Chen's poor morals was mine. Our children are a reflection of ourselves. It was impossible to differentiate which wounded the most: the grief for having a child leave or having an adult child with deplorable morals.

Upon Hildah's return, we had a family feast. Pointing to the excellence of my children, she told me I was a wonderful Mother. Nodding towards her upright son Jacob, a young man with unquestioned probity, I responded to Hildah she was also a terrific Mother. "We can privately congratulate ourselves without seeming proud," I told her, "and you deserve it. But I feel like a terribly ineffective Mother because of what Chen did."

Hildah replied, "we raised our children up in The LORD and we are grateful for how they turned out. You nurtured and corrected them all in the same manner.

Chazaq, Lena and Susanna are exemplary people. Chen turned from his raising. It's not your fault, yet you are allowing him to become an idol."

"An idol?"

"Indeed. You dwell on Chen night and day."

"How can I refrain? I do not know where he is. I don't know if he's safe. I don't know what he is doing. He left our LORD and our family."

"Jehovah El Roi is the one who sees. He sees Chen right now. Is The LORD'S hand so short He cannot reach your son? This situation with Chen is an idol in your life."

"I don't understand what you are saying. Your father, mother, and husband died. I admired how you endured so faithfully. But in this situation, my son is alive. Chen is alive, as far as we know, but he left our family and our LORD. Scripture does not address such a situation. How do you expect me to respond?"

My vehement indignation was based on Hildah's wrongful accusation of idolatry. Since Chen's departure, when I lay face down on the floor praying, it felt like a team of oxen were stomping on my back. Hildah suggested The LORD was using this situation to rid the chaff from my life. "I understand the pounding you experience," Hildah said. "When my husband died, it seemed I was on the threshing floor. Yes, I know the feeling of oxen treading across your back, but The LORD uses everything we go through. He makes the bitter thing sweet. You will look back and see the good in this."

Gradually, I admitted to myself and Hildah that Chen had become an idol. He occupied and regulated my thoughts and feelings. This allowance gave great power to the circumstance and permitted it to define and control me.

"I don't want to wallow in self-pity, Hildah. What must I do?"

"Lift up your eyes."

"Lift up your eyes? Why do you continually quote Scripture and try to make connections to my life? Why can't we have a normal conversation?"

"His Word I have hidden in my heart is why. It is in me. The LORD told Abraham to lift up his eyes and this is what you must do."

"So that my descendants will be as the stars? Come on Hildah, this is a stretch."

"Shabar, do you believe The LORD?"

"Certainly I believe in The LORD! You know I do!"

"You believe in The LORD, but do you believe The

LORD?"

"I don't understand the difference."

"I believe in The LORD and I believe what He says. I believe what He says as much as I believe in Him."

"Elaborate, please. Hildah, you know I want to grasp what you are saying, but it seems we are mincing words here."

"The Torah says our father Abraham believed The LORD."

"Why do I think we are going down another grandiose rabbit trail?"

"Because you are trying to reason this out by what you see. As daughters of Abraham, we are in covenant with The LORD. Abraham believed The LORD about having a son twenty-five years before Isaac was born. Likewise, you would do well to believe The LORD."

"What should I believe?"

"You should believe what is written." It was then that Hildah showed me parchments on which she recorded parts of the writings of the prophets. She served in the synagogue and was permitted to sit right outside the room so she could hear instruction for the young men. Hildah took notes from the lectures and studied. Her knowledge of the Scriptures and The LORD was tantamount to an educated man. Few realized her spiritual understanding. On the parchments were Scriptures which Hildah believed had application to her life.

"The LORD speaks through the writings and the prophets and he 'watches over His Word to perform it'. For instance, Isaiah wrote, 'I will pour out My Spirit on your descendants and My blessing on your offspring'. Pray this for Chen and speak it over him. Bear in mind, The Lord spoke creation into existence."

"But Chen is in a faraway land. A woman at the synagogue heard he was beyond the Golan, living wildly with...I don't want to repeat what she told me..."

"Yes, I heard the same foolish gossip, Shabar, and it doesn't matter. Remember, He is The LORD who sees and He is watching over His word to perform it. Think of the many hours Chen spent learning the Scriptures as he grew up. The LORD said His Word would not return void without accomplishing that for which He sent it. To pray and speak over Chen's life it crucial. The LORD hastens His Word to perform it."

"Pray and speak over Chen's life?"

"Of course. The LORD *spoke* the earth into creation. To speak His Word over situations is powerful. Words we speak are significant. King Solomon proclaimed, 'The power over life and death is in the tongue' and held we are ensnared by the words of our mouths. Jacob and Rachel are a good example of that."

"What about Jacob and Rachel?"

"Recall, Jacob did not know Rachel took her father's idols. When Laban questioned, Jacob said the person who took the gods 'shall not live'. Soon after, Rachel died in child birth."

"I know these writings are in the Tanakh, but Chen left our LORD and I do not see how the words we speak applies to this situation. Do you think there is hope for him? What if he is worshipping false gods with gentiles and pagans?"

"Yes, I do believe there is hope for Chen. Job wrote, 'I know my Redeemer lives'. Let's focus our minds on The LORD, not on what Chen did and may or not be doing. Our Redeemer lives and he is in the business of redeeming people and lives."

"But the Messiah has not appeared on earth?"

"Scripture states our Redeemer lives and He can redeem this circumstance. Focus on Him!"

"Do you believe Chen may possibly return to our God and our family? He would never be accepted in the synagogue and I'm not sure Saul would receive him. He will not speak of Chen."

"Yes, I believe it is possible, but these are matters which you must take to The LORD in the *Secret Place*. I declare nothing is too hard for Him!"

"How and where shall I find the *Secret Place*, Hildah?"

"The *Secret Place* is communion with The LORD from your innermost being. Ask The LORD, Shabar. He will give you the answers you seek and show you great and mighty things which you do not know."

Finally, after many days, I found the *Secret Place*! The physical location was the shady part of the balcony outside my chamber which overlooked our property. Our home, on the shores of the Sea of Galilee, was a Shabbat's walk to the synagogue in Capernaum and our land extended beyond Peniel. I could see far across the land and sea, but no one could see me nestled behind a huge trellis covered with lush fuchsia bougainvilleas. The cold marble floor neutralized the summer heat. Aromas from olive and pomegranate trees floated in the breeze. It was common to see Saul gazing north towards the Golan. We never conversed about Chen's return, but it seemed he was watching for our son. Many hours of each day I spent reading, copying and memorizing Hildah's notes.

Encounters with The LORD were as real to me as with people and frequently I resented their intrusions. Fasting intensified time spent with The LORD and the Scriptures jumped off the parchment at me. His "words were sweeter than honey to my mouth" and I could not wait to borrow the next. I began serving at the synagogue with Hildah because I craved His Word. I wanted to be with Him and near Him. Painful desperation led to the most amazing and rewarding time of my life.

How did The LORD become my friend? *My* friend? It took a while before I felt this was not irreverent, recalling Rabbi Hokhmah emphasized The LORD created Adam because he was lonely. Why did The LORD want to spend time with me? Because I was His daughter. The prophets in their writings asserted The LORD is our Father. I loved Chen despite the choices he made. I realized The LORD loved me unconditionally. He loved me when I was jealous, bitter and selfish. As the love I held for my son, The LORD could not love me more and he did not love me less. Some at the synagogue would stone me for expressing this. Hildah and Rabbi Hokhmah, however, told me I was exactly right. Delighting myself in The LORD was not a work, it was a relationship. The desire of my heart was sweet communion with The LORD.

Bored with daily prayers for Chen's protection and well-being, I heeded Hildah's advice to pray Scriptures over my son. Why not pray huge prayers? Examining Joel's writings, I prayed my son would "prophesy and see visions". Hildah was right. Nothing was too hard for The LORD!

Each day brought a new Scripture to pray for Chen. To paraphrase Isaiah's writing, I spoke, "my son Chen will feast on the inheritance of Jacob his father. The mouth of The LORD has spoken."

Another day I applied Isaiah's writing, "I will pour out my Spirit on your offspring, and My blessing on your descendants." Into Scriptures I continually inserted Chen's name.

Tough times intermingled with blessings. Nightmares and panic attacks were fewer and less intense. On the seventh Passover since Chen's departure, I felt quite disheartened and spiraled down into sorrow. In fact, there were many days of discouragement and longing. It seemed The LORD did not hear my prayers and had no compassion for me. Often I felt I could not continue in my circumstance, but when I focused my mind on The LORD, He kept me in perfect peace. I was revived when I went back and read excerpts and Scriptures from my journal. Is this how King David encouraged himself in The LORD, I wondered?

Writings about waiting on The LORD came to my mind. King David described his experiences of waiting for The LORD. Hosea believed we should wait for The LORD continually. Isaiah contended waiting would renew our strength. Similarly, Jeremiah opined The LORD is good to those who wait for Him. Waiting was beneficial for these great men of God. Therefore, I hoped there was purpose in my sorrow and waiting.

Waiting! I felt stuck in a valley of pain and trouble. Waiting on The LORD was excruciatingly difficult. One day, He brought to my remembrance Hosea's writing, "There I will (...) make the Valley of Achor a door of hope." Somehow, The LORD was transforming this lowest time of trouble to a door of hope. Again, Hildah was correct. The LORD spoke to me through His Word as lucidly as Rabbi Hokhmah and others. For the darkest days when I did not think I could take another step, His Word was a light unto my feet.

Another day, in the *Secret Place*, The LORD dealt with me about judging others. With most human encounters, as Chief Judger, I habitually and instantaneously formed an opinion by internally evaluating perceived shortcomings. Few met my arrogant standards, which under the present condition were cracked and crumbled like tent fabric worn by the desert sun. My attitude towards poor people was condescending because I presumed they were lazy and not living right. Anyone with a wayward child unquestionably possessed major deficits in character. Deeply embedded in this thinking was that people with problems were receiving their deserved punishment. Such reflection broke my heart as I plunged from a fragile, self-constructed, lofty perch. Some may say I tumbled off my high camel.

Intimate encounters with The LORD produced compassion and unfamiliar empathy. I realized the most annoying and off putting women at the synagogue, the most difficult to love, were the ones who needed love the most. Harlots I now regarded as desperate women with deep, outwardly unperceivable wounds who knew no other way to survive. Under different life circumstances, I may have found myself making the same choices. They did not understand how much The LORD loved them and I began to join Hildah in demonstrations of kindness and help.

The relationship with my husband also improved. Saul did not know why I stayed such long hours on my balcony, but he seemed pleased with the reduced nagging and content to leave well enough alone.

Soon The LORD brought Jochebed, Moses' mother, to my mind. My conversation with The LORD about her was most delightful. Wow! She had no control over her son, but placed him in the river, *surrendering* her child to The LORD. I would never have done that, except in her case, it was necessary to spare his life. I clung tightly to my son, to protect and manipulate good things for him. Was that wrong? Of course not. The LORD and I went on and on.

Eventually I heard, *"surrender"*. It was an inaudible voice, but it resounded as clearly as I ever heard anything. I discerned it involved Chen, but what did The LORD want me to *surrender*?

Like Hannah, I cried and begged The LORD for a son. Although I couldn't leave him in the Temple, I dedicated Chen to The LORD in my heart. When he dropped out of Rabbinical studies we were disappointed, but pleased to have him join the family enterprise. I dedicated Chen to The LORD, but did not know how to *surrender* my son.

I was amenable to The LORD, but my son left! What

was there to *surrender*? What did *surrender* entail? The flood gate opened. Anger, hurt, rejection, self-hatred, judgment, fear, envy and resentment for the success and well-being of other peoples' children. I giggled and asked The LORD if he wanted me to continue. He did. There was a subtle grudge towards Saul because he did not act and communicate the way I wanted him to respond. Disinterested in my other children, I treated them and their families with indifference. Habitually, I was more preoccupied with my reputation and what others were thinking than I concerned myself with The LORD. The attitudes which needed to change were enormously overwhelming and would take time. I wanted to *surrender*, but did not know how. For the time being, the idea was placed on hold.

While in prayer the following evening, The LORD brought forgiveness to my mind. Actually it was forgiveness and unforgiveness. Forgiveness? Unforgiveness? Well at least it was not *surrender* again, which was a relief, but I wasn't aware of anyone I needed to forgive. "Whom do I need to forgive? Against whom am I harboring unforgiveness?" I asked my LORD.

His answer seemed multitudinous. I needed to forgive my husband, myself, and everyone else in the world with children who loved them and their LORD. For what did I need to forgive Saul? Why did I need to forgive myself? On the surface it was illogical, but I needed to forgive Saul for not communicating and loving me the way I wished. I needed to forgive myself for not being perfect.

The LORD revealed deeply entrenched bitterness and resentment towards people with happy families who walked in His ways. Moreover, through incongruent tears and laughter, I was impressed to forgive The LORD for allowing this circumstance. You my LORD? Really, I need to forgive my LORD? The LORD of course did not need my forgiveness and I would later understand.

Hildah giggled when I told her about the need to forgive my wonderful husband. Along with everyone else she thought Saul was the greatest and said forgiveness was to release him from unrealistic expectations. She believed the act of forgiveness for practically the entire world was to divest myself of bitterness and resentment towards others whom I perceived had a better life. She confirmed my thinking that forgiveness extended towards The LORD was figuratively to cleanse my heart from wrong, latent thoughts that Chen's departure was for my punishment.

Hildah agreed I needed to forgive myself for self-hatred with not being perfect. Again, it was to cleanse my heart. The LORD told me it was vital to love myself because He created me in His image. If The LORD loved me I could love myself. This gave revelation to the commandment about loving my neighbor as myself. I could not fully love others until I loved myself. It was imperative.

Because the Messiah, Emmanuel, had not yet appeared, I purposed to consult with Rabbi Hokhmah about atonement for my sins, primarily unforgiveness. He and Hildah would know what to do. When we met, there was agreement I should ask Saul to prepare a sacrifice.

Afterwards, Rabbi Hokhmah shared our feast. He was a frequent and pleasant guest, visiting more often since his wife died three years ago. His sons were rabbis in other cities and Hildah held a special affection in his heart. It was widely held that he was assigned to our synagogue years ago, because the Pharisees in Jerusalem thought he lacked the proper temperament to interact with those who served on the Sanhedrin. Reportedly, they wanted Rabbi Hokhmah far away. One of my husband's closest friends, Saul privately expressed he was too cheerful for the group at headquarters. He was a happy man whose loving demeanor enticed us to learn and understand the Torah and the writings.

Soon, in the *Secret Place*, The LORD entreated to revisit the issue of *surrender*. Moses' mother *surrendered* him, but my LORD, I could not put my son in a basket of reeds. Flummoxed, I asked Hildah what *surrendering* Chen meant? Together we answered the question, "The LORD will reveal." Fellowship with Hildah grew sweeter as we shared a diligent pursuit of The LORD.

Surrender. How could I *surrender* an adult child? Many days passed without insight from The LORD. *Fear*, however, returned. It began with the "what if's" in my mind. Hildah encouraged hopefulness that Chen would return, but the "what if's" harassed me. One day, in my *Secret Place* The LORD reminded of King David's writing, "He prepares a table for me in the presence of my enemies." It was a lit candle moment. The King likely was writing about armies, but my chief enemy was *fear* and it all started when my mind turned from The LORD to all the terrible things that could happen to Chen and that I might never see him again.

The *fears* were not unfounded. He was in a faraway land, presumably engaging in risky, even dangerous behaviors among heathens. What if he was harmed? What if he married a foreign wife? What if he fathered heathen children who were not careful to follow the Torah? What if he never came back? Worst, what if his soul was condemned to the wicked part of sheol? The LORD prepared a table in the presence of my enemy, *fear.*

On my table was a feast of Scriptures which I had memorized. Among them was Isaiah's writing, "...do not *fear*, for I am with you; do not be dismayed, for I am your God. I will strengthen you and help you; I will uphold you with my righteous right hand." Familiar was the terror of waking up with nightmares in the middle of the night and the arrow that flew by day assaulted with frightening thoughts and panic. King David's terror and *fears* were different from mine, but I related to his writing, which was a morsel of the feast The LORD prepared for me. I experienced *fear* and refuge in The LORD similarly to King David. I identified with the table The LORD prepared for him. The table He prepared for me was in the *Secret Place*, under the shadow of His wings. Periods of glorious victory notwithstanding, to my consternation, daily battles were too often lost to *fear*.

The next evening, I again heard *"surrender"*. Perplexed, Hildah and I counseled with Rabbi Hokhmah for revelation on how to *surrender* Chen. He recounted how our father Abraham laid Isaac on the altar, in an act of *surrender*.

"Rabbi, I know *surrender* is connected to my son, but I cannot take him to an altar on Mount Moriah. I cannot send him down the river in a basket. This notion perplexes me."

"No you cannot physically do these things, but I believe The LORD is leading you deeper and deeper in an understanding of Himself," Rabbi Hokhmah responded. "Indeed, I think The LORD is leading you to totally *surrender* your life. He is inviting Shabar, not requiring."

"How do you say He invites and does not require?"

"There were two trees in the garden, Shabar. The LORD prizes our free will and offers a choice."

He recommended a template by which Hildah may lead me through a symbolic laying of Chen and other situations on the altar. I left with muddled thoughts of Isaac on the altar and free will, perplexed as ever.

Hildah joined me in my *Secret Place*. Adhering to Rabbi Hokhmah's guidance, she proposed the balcony rail would serve as an altar and flower petals would represent Chen and others areas of my life. On the altar I would place a blossom to denote each issue.

She asked, "Does The LORD have your permission to do or not do anything He chooses in this situation with Chen?"

"What about the promises of God? He watches over His Word to perform it."

"Does The LORD have your permission?"

"The LORD does not need my permission."

"Of course He does not, but does He have it?"

"Well, it's not in my control anyway. That is one thing I have learned."

"But is it okay with you, however this journey ends?"

"Hildah, if you recollect, it was you who encouraged me to have faith in the promises. You taught me to speak and pray Scriptures over Chen. Now you are asking me if it is okay if the promises are not realized. I'm as confused as ever and no, after being built up in the Scripture, it is not okay."

"I understand, Shabar. We can resume this conversation later, when you are ready."

Left alone with The LORD, I told Him, "that will be never".

"Do you trust me?" The LORD asked.

"You are Elohim, The LORD, the maker of heaven and earth...myself and my son."

"So why can't you place Chen on the altar?"

"My LORD, the Scriptures record many calamities You allowed. If I put Chen on the altar, something tragic could happen."

"So you will hold Chen securely in your hand? You will protect him?"

"Yes, my LORD." As I listened to myself, I acknowledged the ludicrous reasoning. "No, my LORD, I cannot hold onto my son when I do not know where he is and You can wipe us all out at any moment."

"I desire mercy, not judgment, Shabar. Have I not demonstrated I AM close to the brokenhearted?"

"Yes, my LORD, so why do you ask me to lay Chen on an altar? It activates every 'what if' and *fear*."

"It does, I know, My beloved. 'Trust in The LORD with all your heart and lean not on your own understanding'."

"Dear LORD, I do trust you with all my heart and I don't lean on my own understanding. My father Abraham was a great patriarch when he laid Isaac on the altar. You know I am a wife and mother. I can't understand this altar activity, that is for certain. Shall I ask Saul to prepare a sacrifice?"

"No, beloved. You will understand in time. Go, take your rest."

Rest I did, with the realization and acceptance of failure to maximize my spiritual potential, but secure in The LORD'S mercy. His anger did not burn against me, but he soon brought *surrender* back to my mind. He knew I did not get it.

Several nights later, during the fourth watch, I awakened with an urgency to go out to the *Secret Place*. Staring at the water, illumined by innumerable stars, I asked, "What is it my LORD, what is it you want me to hear?"

"Can you trust Me?"

"LORD, I don't understand. I want to give the correct answer, but You know I am a simple woman who cannot comprehend what You ask of me."

"Recall the Scriptures. Recall what is written."

"Well, since the Scriptures are vast, could you please be more specific?"

"Our subject is trust. Recall what I spoke to Joshua before he crossed the Jordan."

"With all holy reverence, my LORD, I do not understand how your message to Joshua is pertinent. I do however, feel like I am going on a journey without leaving my home. I am going somewhere unknown and and it is scary. I do not want to go."

"Recall what I spoke to Joshua before he crossed the Jordan."

"'Be strong and of good courage; do not be afraid, do not be dismayed, for the LORD your God is with you wherever you go,' but my LORD this is odd. I already live in Capernaum, which is across the Jordan."

"This writing is for you, Shabar. Recall others about *fear* and trust."

I remembered King Solomon wrote, "trust in The LORD with all your heart". The Psalmist declared, "those who trust in The LORD shall be like Mount Zion, which cannot be shaken."

"Can you trust Me?"

Relenting, I responded, "Yes, my LORD, I do trust

you in my mind. King Solomon exhorted to trust You with all our heart, but that is where *fear* resides. It occupies my heart. I trust You in my mind, an intellectual assent, but I confess I don't trust You with all my heart. Anyway, my LORD, the earth is your footstool and we are like grasshoppers. Why does it matter if I trust You?"

"You may not feel you can trust Me, but you can make a decision to trust Me. You are partnering with *fear*, which is tyrannizing your life. *Fear* is a cruel master. As an act of your will, you can choose to trust Me and place Chen on the altar."

The altar again. I hoped The LORD had forgotten. Incapable to break through, I shared my encounter with The LORD to Hildah at daybreak. She accompanied me to the synagogue to seek counsel from Rabbi Hokhmah. "What must I do? How may I comprehend?" Hildah sat behind us, silently interceding.

"The LORD understands you are afraid to trust Him".

"I *do* trust The LORD and why is it so important anyway?"

"Because you cannot enjoy the fullness of intimacy with The LORD if you do not trust Him. He wants to relieve you of the bondage to *fear*."

Frustrated and confused as ever, I wept.

"This is *total surrender*, Shabar. The LORD is asking this of you because it is His best for you. When you choose to *surrender* Chen as a decision of your will, your emotions will follow. You will no longer be tormented by *fear*, panic and nightmares. Don't worry. We are not going to pluck out your gut and jump up and down on it."

"How did you know that is what I am feeling?"

"It is how we all felt. You will feel differently this evening, however, because your emotions will no longer dominate. You will see. This will help you," he assured.

"So the process of symbolically placing Chen on the altar is to activate a decision of my will?" The peculiar activity was gradually making sense.

"Yes, my daughter." Rabbi Hokhmah plucked several branches from a Rose of Sharon and motioned into the synagogue. Using the same format as Hildah, he said the bench would figuratively serve as an altar. "Now," he said, "to assuage the enormity of the powerful emotions you are experiencing, I will structure our time and lead you in *surrender* as a decision of your will. Shabar, I ask you to repeat after me."

"But you told me The LORD did not cause this situation."

"A bit off topic, Shabar, but no, The LORD did not cause your situation. He allowed the circumstance into your life. Also, He gave Chen a free will. Let's move forward."

"But what about the promises of The LORD regarding my son?"

"Those will be on the altar as well, Shabar."

Following his lead, as Hildah persevered with quiet intercession, I surrendered grief, plans and dreams for my son. Each petal represented a *fear*, a hope or a regret. On the altar were control, rejection, pride, self-hatred, envy and many emotions I thought were gone. Lastly I chose to *surrender* the promises of the Scriptures and it was okay, by a decision of my will, if they never came to pass. Acknowledging Chen was The LORD's son, I conceded He could do with his life and this circumstance as He chose. I gave up the right to have promises fulfilled, after all, they were HIS promises. Rabbi Hokhmah was correct. I left a son I could not hold and a burden I could not carry on the altar that day.

My agenda, reputation, desires and aspirations were abandoned at the altar. Empty of myself, I was overcome by His Spirit and full of His power. The LORD'S presence permeated my being. I will take being overcome by His Spirit rather than being filled with self-pity, self-doubt, self-loathing (do we see a pattern here?), pride and insecurity any day.

Unable to raise myself from the synagogue floor, exhaustion and invigoration dueled to define my condition.

The meticulously designed, tenuous stone exterior, years under development, was demolished during two watches. Recapturing the former toxic emotions, judgments, habits and unhealthy thought patterns was as futile as isolating and extracting every particle of salt from the Dead Sea. It could not be done.

I now understood The LORD'S reference to Joshua crossing the Jordan. The experience of *total surrender* was like entering a personal promised land. For the rubbish and dross I left on the altar, The LORD exchanged the sensation of a well-watered garden, as Isaiah described, like a spring whose waters never fail. He granted rest, peace and joy unspeakable. Rabbi Hokhmah and Hildah said they discerned the ubiquitous presence of the Holy Spirit in the synagogue. They were thankful and praising The Lord for what He did and expressed their delight for me.

I did not immediately share with Saul because he was lovingly disengaged from personal insight or emotionally evocative conversation. That was fine because he and our relationship were on the altar as well!

As many Shabbats passed, I was able to genuinely live above the circumstance of having and missing a Prodigal Son. Without ceasing I thanked The LORD for His presence and asked what He wanted to teach me in and through emotionally challenging days. What did He want me to know? This was a time of vast learning. Despite the unchanging circumstance or what I was feeling, peace, joy and transparency radiated from the *Secret Place* to my family and others.

One day, suddenly, as I was playing with my grandchildren on the balcony, I heard a commotion from Saul. Moments later, I saw my dignified husband a long way off, running towards our son. As the curious children scurried downstairs to investigate the excitement, I lingered on the balcony to thank and praise The LORD. I observed Saul embracing Chen and his exuberant call for a celebration. In addition to a robe, he directed the servants to place a signet ring on Chen's finger and sandals on his feet.

There are no words to describe the desires of my heart coming to fruition before my eyes; though it had been years, the Word of The LORD runs swiftly came to mind. Waiting was never easy, but it was worth it. Commensurate with my ecstasy over Chen's return was my gratitude for life changing encounters with The LORD.

With one exception, our family feasted, danced and rejoiced with exceeding merriment. Chazaq was troubled when Saul embraced his brother and conferred instantaneous acceptance back into the family. Saul not only accepted, he honored Chen.

Many perceive Chazaq as petulant, but his initial reaction was understandable. I searched and found him behind the house, venting to Jacob. Hildah's son was a good listener and an adept peacemaker. He understood both sides. For our culture, my husband's behavior was unthinkably inappropriate. I conveyed empathy, affirmation, love and respect for my oldest son. There was abiding rest in the certainty The LORD would heal the conflict between my sons. In due season, both would experience our Father's extravagant love.

My Witness

So you see my sisters, I am part of the great cloud of witnesses who cheer you on during the most exciting time to be alive. A season in which you await the second coming of Messiah, The LORD Jesus, preceded by the greatest harvest of souls ever known.

Your resources are amazing! The written New Testament explains the new covenant, your identity in

Christ and what is to come. The complete Word of God is accessible on your phone whereas we had to go to the synagogue and receive permission to study and review.

Through the Word, you understand what the Blood of Christ accomplished. While we had visitations from the Holy Spirit, Luke's gospel explains He will baptize you with the Holy Spirit and fire. Paul's writings explain you were sealed by the Holy Spirit and your body is His temple. Holy and blameless you are! In these last days, you are partakers of His divine nature and may come boldly to the throne of grace! In Yeshua, you move and breathe and have your being.

Rabbi Hokhmah led me to *totally surrender* my life to purge toxic thoughts and emotions, but you now understand this is identification with The LORD Jesus, who gave up his right as a deity to come to earth as a man. Christ is your life. As you give up your rights and *totally surrender*, you understand the great exchange which took place when our Savior died on the cross for us all.

There is a plethora of Word teaching churches from which to choose. How about Christian radio in your cars? More astonishing, there are anointed women, including Marilyn Hickey, Joyce Meyer and Beth Moore who teach multitudes around the world.

Paradoxically, however, your path is more challenging because you know more and the world is rapidly changing to advance towards the apex of history. All the information, not to be confused with wisdom, in the world is available with a click. Creation is groaning and creating stress that was absent from my simpler time. Nuclear weapons loom. Your husbands are bombarded with sensuality, temptation and perversion, the repercussions of which many families suffer. Your children and adolescents can access the same topics on the internet and other media. As well, many modern women have exciting, challenging careers. There is an expectation to excel professionally and maintain an unrealistic standard of beauty and body image, all whilst fulfilling the role of perfect wife and Mother.

Still, life is life and we cope with similar spiritual and emotional challenges in our relationships with families and friends. As a progenitor, my story is a gift of comfort and encouragement to others who find themselves walking the path of the Prodigal Mother.

Epilogue

Three years after Chen's return to our family, Jesus from Nazareth based his ministry in Capernaum and taught in our synagogue. Chen was drawn to Jesus from the beginning and spent much time helping Him and the disciples as they went about Galilee. Chazaq and Jacob eagerly took up his responsibilities for the family business because he brought back Jesus' teachings and life to the rest of us. He loved traveling with them, especially John. Once, after Jesus spoke about His Father in heaven, Chen shared his testimony about how Saul demonstrated and extended the Father's unconditional, undeserved love to him.

When we met Jesus and heard Him speak, we believed He was the Son of God. Significant miracles were performed here and it was our privilege to extend hospitality. Chen followed the group to Bethany and Jerusalem. He sent word of Jesus' crucifixion, resurrection and ascension and reported the coming of the Holy Spirit in the Upper Room. It was after these events in Jerusalem that Rabbi Hokhmah explained how Jesus fulfilled the Law and the writings of the prophets.

Rabbi Hokhmah spent the remainder of his ministry preaching the good news about Jesus. Chen assisted and taught when he was not away on mission trips.

My relationship with Saul? The LORD definitely saved the best wine for the last!

Judy Wills Lowder

Encouragements

Through thirty years in counseling practice, Prodigal Mothers are amongst my most frequent clients. Therefore, when I considered the parable, I wondered about the Mother. Where was she? What was she doing? I speculate she was in her *Secret Place*, travailing in intercession, standing in the gap, praying and speaking the Word over the circumstances. She probably waited a long time, as the Prodigal Son returned only after he squandered his inheritance. Likely the Prodigal Mother was on her face before the Lord, interceding for her Prodigal Son, older son and her husband. Mothers are like that, aren't we?

The following encouragements contain carefully disguised situations which were encountered through friendships, acquaintances or clients. If you think you may recognize a person, you are wrong! Each situation is an amalgamation of circumstances. Bits and pieces are scrambled to protect confidentiality. Who knows, maybe some are made up to illustrate a point. Perhaps there is a situation to which you can relate and hopefully these verses and meditations will minister to you.

Salient Verses

For God so loved the world that He gave His one and only Son, that whoever believes in Him shall not perish but have eternal life.
John 3:16

He will baptize you with the Holy Spirit and fire.
Luke 3:16

Whoever believes in me, as Scripture has said, rivers of living water will flow from within them.
John 7:38

I am crucified with Christ: nevertheless, I live; yet not I, but Christ liveth in me: and the life which I now live in the flesh I live by the faith of the Son of God, who loved me, and gave himself for me.
Galatians 2:20 (KJV)

The Spirit and the Bride say, "Come!" And let anyone who hears say, "Come!" Let the one who is thirsty come; and let the one who wishes take the free gift of the water of life.
Revelation 22:1

Judy Wills Lowder

The Secret Place

He who dwells in the secret place of the Most High
Shall abide under the shadow of the Almighty.
I will say of The LORD, "He is my refuge and my fortress;
My God; in Him will I trust."
Surely he shall deliver you from the snare of the fowler
And from the perilous pestilence.
He shall cover you with his feathers,
And under his wings you shall take refuge;
His truth shall be your shield and buckler.
You shall not be afraid of the terror by night
Nor of the arrow that flies by day,
Nor of the pestilence that walks in darkness,
Nor of the destruction that lays waste at noonday.
A thousand may fall at your side,
And ten thousand at your right hand;
But it shall not come near you.
Only with your eyes shall you look,
And see the reward of the wicked.
Because you have made The LORD, who is my refuge,
Even the Most High, your dwelling place,
No evil shall befall you,
Nor shall any plague come near your dwelling;
For He shall give His angels charge over you,
To keep you in all your ways.
In their hands they shall bear you up,
Lest you dash your foot against a stone.
You shall tread upon the lion and the cobra,

*The young lion and the serpent you shall trample
underfoot.
"Because he has set his love upon Me,
therefore, I will deliver him;
I will set him on high, because he has known My name.
He shall call upon Me, and I will answer him,
I will be with him in trouble;
I will deliver him and honor him
With long life I will satisfy him,
And show him My salvation."*

Psalm 91 (New King James Version)

1

Let's consider Shabar's progression towards spiritual and emotional well-being:

- She felt her pain. Shabar did not numb the pain with alcohol or food. At times it was unbearable and she considered fleeing to another village, but she persevered and continuously brought her hurts to The LORD.
- Shabar engaged and treasured the fellowship of her Word believing sister and mentor.
- Shabar hungered after, believed and appropriated God's Word for her life.
- Shabar fasted. She prayed God's Word over the circumstance.
- She was sensitive to the leading of the Spirit of God. (Hildah personified the role of the Holy Spirit in our lives.)
- Shabar sought wisdom from her spiritual leader, Rabbi Hokhmah.
- She looked to The LORD, not only her husband, to meet her needs. Saul was supportive,

but it is humanly impossible for another person to mend our deep hurts and fulfill all our emotional needs.

• Shabar learned how to encourage herself in The LORD.

• Shabar discovered the *Secret Place* (Psalm 91).

• Shabar confessed her sins and fears to The LORD. She was transparent about her reluctance to totally surrender her life.

• She incrementally and authentically advanced towards total surrender. Shabar had to process her fears and rest in The LORD's unconditional love before she could completely yield her life. The Holy Spirit engineers our circumstances and gently brings us to total surrender.

2

The Great Exchange which occurred on the Cross defines and informs our Christian walk:

- Eternal life for spiritual death
- Victory for defeat
- Purity for filth
- Wisdom for foolishness
- Freedom for bondage
- Health for sickness
- Peace for panic
- Trust for fear
- Understanding for ignorance
- Joy for depression
- Beauty for ashes
- Calm for anxiety
- Dancing for mourning
- Mercy for judgment
- Forgiveness for wrath
- His righteousness for self-righteousness
- Agape love for self-loathing
- Rest for labor

- Patience for edginess
- Kindness for malice
- Gentleness for harshness
- Self-control for indulgence
- Abundance for lack
- His strength for our weakness
- Sleep for insomnia
- Clarity for confusion
- The mind of Christ for mental illness
- A sound mind (sozo) for emotional instability
- Truth for lies
- Calm for stress
- Kindness for malice
- Pleasure for bitterness
- Praise for offense

What else did Jesus exchange for you on the Cross?

3

The Prodigal Father

An examination of the Prodigal Father's actions reflect the heart of Papa God. A friend who temporarily worked in China told me the Scripture is known as the Parable of the Loving Father in the region he visited. Saul was a bit too passive for Shabar, but she never impugned his character. As she grew in The LORD, she acknowledged she expected too much. A nobleman, Saul was dignified. Shabar described the area of their land and he was exceedingly prosperous.

Saul's response to Chen was characteristic of Papa's heart. Below are examples.

Saul let his son go. Rather than keep Chen against his will, he released him. Chen's request for his inheritance was comparable to wishing his father dead. He could not wait. He wanted his bounty now and Saul complied to the worst insult a child could give a parent. The LORD loves us, permits our free will and allows us to pursue things that keep us from our destiny.

Saul apparently prayed and anticipated Chen's return, for when he saw Chen a far way off he ran to him. This was unusual because men in Middle Eastern culture typically do not run. Jesus intercedes for us and the Holy Spirit pursues. The LORD chases us with unconditional love.

The robe evoked the garment of salvation and the robe of righteousness The LORD bestows upon us. It also represented protection. The robe signified Chen was back under the protection of the family.

The signet ring sealed Chen's reinstatement as a family member. It represents his identity as a son, which Saul restored. Our identity is in Christ.

Servants during this time went barefoot. When Saul had sandals placed on Chen's feet it designated full benefits as a son. Saul wanted his son back, not another servant.

The feast celebrated life and the reunification of the family. The fatted calf was a fine meal on a festive occasion. The Prodigal Father not only received the son back, he celebrated him. The Prodigal Son was honored and lavished with love.

This is the author's creative interpretation of the parable. It is not a theological discourse or extra Biblical thesis.

For this son of mine was dead and he is alive again; he was lost and is found.
Luke 15: 24

Judy Wills Lowder

Surely your goodness and unfailing love will pursue me all the days of my life, and I will live in the house of the LORD forever.
Psalm 23:6 (NLT)

For He has clothed me with the garments of salvation, He has covered me with the robe of righteousness.
Isaiah 61:10 (NKJV)

The Spirit you received brought about your adoption to sonship. And by Him, we cry, Abba, Father.
Romans 8:15

I have loved you with an everlasting love.
Jeremiah 31:3

4

The Vine

In my native Georgia, we grow tons of tomatoes. Close inspection of mature plants reveal it is practically impossible to determine the vine from the branches, which are entangled and twisted together. A branch broken off from the vine will wither and die. Likewise, with grapevines. It is the same with us and The LORD. When we are in Christ, our lives are enmeshed with His. He is our life and it is impossible to separate ourselves from Him.

I am the vine; you are the branches, if you remain in me and I in you, you will bear much fruit; apart from me you can do nothing.
John 15:5

On that day you will realize that I am in my Father, and you are in me, and I am in you.
John 14:20

When Christ, who is our life, appears, then you also will appear with him in glory.
Colossians 3:4

Judy Wills Lowder

5

No Greater Joy

The Prodigal Mother of a highly successful son described the situation. At age 22, he was the youngest person ever selected to an executive training program for an international company. Completely indifferent to The LORD, he expressed religion was for the weak and uneducated. The Prodigal Mother wept over her "trophy" son, saying all she ever wanted for her children was to love The LORD. She was often congratulated for her child's achievement and success, but it was rubbish to her, compared to walking in Christ. Not all prodigals are down and out. Everything else was in vain for this Prodigal Mother if her son rejected Christ. She made a decision to believe God's Word and committed to pray her son would know the truth and the truth would set him free. She prayed for no greater joy than knowing her son walked in the Truth.

I am the way and the truth and the life.
John 14:6

Then you will know the truth, and the truth will set you free.
John 8:32

I have no greater joy than to hear that my children are walking in the truth.
1 John 3:4

6

The Saddest Prodigal Mother

Was not one. During a visit to Germany, a sad, elderly lady told me of many problems with her adult children and grandchildren. When I asked if I could pray for her, she declined, saying, "that is for the young people. It's too late for me." She would not pray with me at the moment, but I later prayed for her.

No, it is never too late to receive the salvation of The LORD. A Mother or Grandmother can come boldly to the throne of grace to intercede for children and grandchildren.

I will pour out my Spirit on your offspring, and my
blessing on your descendants.
Isaiah 44:3

Let us then approach God's throne of grace with
confidence, so that we may receive mercy and find grace to
help us in our time of need.
Hebrews 4:16

Even to your old age and gray hairs I am he, I am he who will sustain you. I have made you and I will carry you; I will sustain you and I will rescue you.
Isaiah 46:4

7

Don't Forsake Your Own

Her son was in jail for stealing in order to obtain more drugs. The Prodigal Mother did not want to go see him. Instead of a visit she reasoned she would fast and pray, leaving her son exiled, alone in the cell with The LORD. Surely he would hear The LORD speaking to him. Previously the Prodigal Mother served in a prison ministry. As she read Isaiah 58, she realized she had done for others what she would not do for her own son and changed her mind. During her visit, she found an amenable son who wanted to talk about The LORD. He was reading a Bible and grateful for the time she spent with him.

Is not this the kind of fasting I have chosen:
to loose the chains of injustice and untie the cords of the yoke,
to set the oppressed free and break every yoke?
Is it not to share your food with the hungry and to provide the poor wanderer with shelter –
When you see the naked, to clothe them,
And not to turn away from your own flesh and blood?

*Then your light will break forth like the dawn, and your
healing will quickly appear;
Then your righteousness will go before you, and the glory of
The LORD will be your rear guard.
Then you will call, and The LORD will answer; you will
cry for help, and he will say: Here am I.*
Isaiah 58:6-9

8

Surrender the Past

An adolescent, prayed for and loved by a Prodigal Mother, put the family through pain, financial distress and humiliation for several years. It was dire enough that his sister was frightened when he was in the home. The behavior improved, but the Prodigal Mother and her husband felt like they had PTSD from the chaos his raucous living brought upon the family. During a Sunday sermon, her Pastor exhorted the congregation to surrender the past. How, she asked, could she surrender the roller coaster ride her family had endured? She found the answer in the Word.

Not that I have already obtained all this, or have already arrived at my goal, but I press on to take hold of that for which Christ Jesus took hold of me. Brothers and sisters, I do not consider myself yet to have taken hold of it. But one thing I do: Forgetting what is behind and straining toward what is ahead.
Philippians 3:12-13

See! The winter is past; the rains are over and gone.
Flowers appear on the earth the season of singing has come,
the cooing of doves is heard in our land.
Song of Songs 2:11-12

Since, then, you have been raised with Christ, set your
hearts on things above, where Christ is, seated at the right
hand of God.
Colossians 3:1

9

Flaming Arrows

She and her husband served on staff as directors of the college ministry at a large, vibrant church. This Prodigal Mother was deeply distressed because her children, attending out of state universities, were disinterested in The LORD and eschewed Christian activities. Her Prodigals were wandering aimlessly without an academic major or career goals. Both were drinking and partying. One was on academic probation due to excessive revelry. Church members knew the children were straying and her youngest children were ashamed of their older siblings.

She described how difficult her ministry had become. The students in her church were zealous for the presence of The LORD. They were also focused on their programs of study and resolute towards the attainment of professional careers.

Why was this a problem? The Prodigal Mother could almost feel the daggers in her heart as the young people reminded her of everything her children were not. She understood the gossip; her family was in turmoil. As we conversed, she agreed she was experiencing the fiery darts of the enemy.

Fiery darts are intended to discourage and distract us from experiencing The LORD and to hinder our ministry. These fiery darts, flung by the enemy, were accomplishing their purpose! We are directed to extinguish fiery darts with the shield of faith.

When the Prodigal Mother pinpointed the source of her discouragement and The LORD's antidote, she was able to focus on the truth. Over and over she repeated, sometimes aloud, sometimes silently, "I take up the shield of faith and quench every flaming arrow the enemy sends against me." Once again she experienced the joy of ministering to college students and fresh resolve to intercede for her family.

In addition to all this, take up the shield of faith, with which you can extinguish all the flaming arrows of the evil one.
Ephesians 6:16

There is therefore no condemnation for those who are in Christ Jesus.
Romans 8:1

I will pour my Spirit on your offspring, And my blessing on your descendants.
Isaiah 44:3

Judy Wills Lowder

Blessed are those who fear The LORD, who find great delight in His commands. Their children will be mighty in the land.
Psalm 112:1-2

His truth shall be your shield and buckler.
Psalm 91:4

10

His Grace

"Really is sufficient," she said effusively. Everyone knows the often quoted verse. We know it is true because it is the Word. A Prodigal Mother discovered the difference between knowing the Scripture and experiencing the sufficiency of His grace. As she read through a journal from several years past, she realized there was no way she survived except by His grace. Recorded amongst sermons and Bible verses were various crises and spiritual warfare. She was amazed that she not only survived, but formed a new intimacy in her marriage. She earned a significant career promotion during that time as well. This Prodigal Mother encountered the sufficiency of God's grace beyond reading and quoting a verse. She experienced His grace was more than enough to just get by in life.

Three times I pleaded with The LORD to take it from me. But He said to me, "My grace is sufficient for you, for my power is made perfect in weakness."
2 Corinthians 12:8-9

Judy Wills Lowder

May the grace of the Lord Jesus Christ, and the love of God, and the fellowship of the Holy Spirit be with you all.
2 Corinthians 13:14

11

Prepared for the Battle

Many Prodigal Mothers live in unceasing adversity. The LORD allows trials to increase our faith and the capacity to know and serve Him. You have been prepared for this trial because the Word says He will not allow us to endure more than we can handle. Before He allowed this trial, He knew you could persevere and endure. Warrior, you were made for this battle!

No temptation has overtaken you except what is common to mankind. And God is faithful; He will not let you be tempted beyond what you can bear.
1 Corinthians 10:13

Consider it pure joy, my brothers, whenever you face trials of many kinds,
because you know that the testing of your faith develops perseverance.
Perseverance must finish its work so that you may be mature and complete, not lacking anything.
James 1:2-4

Judy Wills Lowder

For God has not given us a spirit of fear, but a spirit of power and love and a sound mind.
2 Timothy 1:7

I am filled with power, with the Spirit of the LORD.
Micah 3:8

Now thanks be unto God, who always causes us to triumph in Christ, and through us diffuses the fragrance of his knowledge in every place.
2 Corinthians 2:14 (NKJV)

…we also glory in our sufferings, because we know that suffering produces perseverance; perseverance, character; and character, hope. And hope does not put us to shame, because God's love has been poured out into our hearts through the Holy Spirit, who has been given to us.
Romans 5:3-5

In all this you greatly rejoice, though now for a little while you may have had to suffer grief in all kinds of trials. These have come so that the proven genuineness of your faith—of greater worth than gold, which perishes even though refined by fire—may result in praise, glory and honor when Jesus Christ is revealed.
1 Peter 1:7

12

Labor to Enter His Rest

To perceive this concept as contradictory is an understatement. After years of praying for her adult child, a Prodigal Mother expressed immense weariness. She said if she could change the situation, she would have changed it a long time ago and if she could rescue her child she would have rescued him a long time ago. The son was caught up in destructive behaviors which included everything by which Prodigals entangle themselves. The Prodigal Mother was spiritually and emotionally depleted.

We recognized she needed to rest in The LORD. An action person, this was inconsistent with her personality. Contemplating the need, we asked The LORD'S guidance and help to enter His rest. If it was easy, He would not have told us to labor.

Let us labor therefore to enter His rest.
Hebrews 4:11 (King James Bible)

Come to Me, all who are weary and burdened, and I will give you rest. Take my yoke upon you and learn from me, for I am gentle and humble in heart, and you will find rest for your souls.
Matthew 11:28-29

This is what the Sovereign LORD, the Holy One of Israel, says: In repentance and rest is your salvation.
Isaiah 30:15

13

Spiritual Warfare

A Prodigal Mother, appalled with her son's despicable behavior and indifference towards the repercussions for the family, was justifiably angry and toiling to offset bitterness. We recollected Paul's writing that our battle is not against flesh and blood; her Prodigal was not the actual enemy. He continues to explain the real battle and how to arm and ready ourselves.

In Ephesians, Paul instructs to put on the full armor of God. Particularly germane to Prodigal Mothers are the helmet of salvation to guard the thoughts, the breastplate of righteousness to protect the emotions and the shield of faith to deflect the flaming arrows discharged by the enemy. He further urges to take up the sword of the Spirit, which is the Word of God; praying always with all prayer and supplication in the Spirit.

Weapons of our warfare include reading and praying the Word, fasting and intercession. We appropriate the weapons through prayer and rest in the knowledge the battle is The LORD'S. Thanksgiving and praise are strategic!

Judy Wills Lowder

*Finally, my brethren, be strong in the LORD and in
the power of His might. Put on the whole armor of God,
that you may be able to withstand against the wiles of the
devil. For we do not wrestle against flesh and blood, but
against principalities, against powers, against the rulers
of the darkness of this age, against spiritual wickedness in
heavenly places.*
Ephesians 6:10-12 (KJV)

*For the weapons of our warfare are not carnal, but mighty
through God to the pulling down of strongholds.*
2 Corinthians 2:4 (King James 2000 Bible)

The prayer of a righteous person is powerful and effective.
James 5:16

*Do not be afraid! Don't be discouraged by this mighty
army, for the battle is not yours, but God's.*
2 Chronicles 20:15

The LORD will fight for you; you need only to be still.
Exodus 14:14

*I will contend with those who contend with you, and your
children I will save.*
Isaiah 49:25

*Enter His gates with thanksgiving and His courts with
praise; give thanks to Him and praise His name.*
Psalm 100:4

14

Grieve Not the Holy Spirit

Desiring answers to her prayers, a Prodigal Mother was trying to perform well and avoid grieving the Holy Spirit. She brought her check list, which included daily devotions and weekly Bible study, for my review. She asked if I thought she was doing everything right. My response was to explain how Jesus accomplished for her each item on the list.

We examined the verse and noted the preceding addressed corrupt communication, not our Christian performance. We realized speaking corrupt communication, along with wrong attitudes towards others, grieves the Holy Spirit. There is caution against such negative commentary as, "he will be a drug addict all his life. I doubt we will ever see him alive again."

Speaking words that are contrary to the Word of God, along with gossip and lying, are corrupt. Let's make sure our words line up with God's words. We edify ourselves when we encourage others.

Judy Wills Lowder

Do not let any unwholesome talk come out of your mouths,
but only what is helpful for building others up according to
their needs, that it may benefit those who listen. And do not
grieve the Holy Spirit of God, with whom you were sealed for
the day of redemption.
Ephesians 4:29-30

The tongue has the power of life and death,
and those who love it will eat its fruit.
Proverbs 18:21

May the words of my mouth and the meditation of my heart
be pleasing in your sight, O LORD,
my Rock and my Redeemer.
Psalm 19:14

15

Treasures Hidden in the Darkness

After weeks of rumination over her son's misbehaviors and how she should have parented differently, she was overwhelmed with a beautiful revelation. This Prodigal Mother expressed how she unexpectedly received a glimpse of The LORD's unconditional love for her.

As she dwelt on her son's devastating lifestyle, she realized she was fearful, hurt and angry because she loved him. Despite his unacceptable choices, her love was unchanged. There was nothing he could do to stifle her love, which was equal to the affection she held for his siblings who were doing well. For the first time, she grasped the enormity of our Father's unconditional love. Agape. None of her failures caused Him to love her less and virtuous behavior did not compel Him to love her more. She could not do better, work harder or give more to increase The LORD'S agape love for her. She loves her son simply because he is her child and therefore understood The LORD loves her simply because she is His daughter .

Judy Wills Lowder

The verse literally refers to hidden gold and wealth during the reign of Cyrus, however, this Prodigal Mother considered the encounter with agape love a treasure she found hidden amidst the darkness of shame, destruction and pain. Delight in Papa's love today.

I will give you hidden treasures, riches stored in secret places, so that you may know that I am the Lord, the God of Israel, who summons you by name.
Isaiah 45:3

16

Total Surrender

When Rabbi Hokhmah led Shabar to surrender her life, it was for her good, to cleanse her heart of fear and grief. She learned to trust The LORD with all her heart and lean not unto her own understanding.

Under the new covenant, we comprehend the incarnation of The LORD Jesus giving up His right as a deity to walk on earth as a human and die a criminal's death on a cross. Total surrender entails undergoing our personal garden of Gethsemane. We identify with The LORD Jesus when we surrender our hopes, plans and dreams to His will. Often we need to yield our reputation, control, relationships and the right to be right. We must relinquish our expectations for others to act and respond in the way we want. The Holy Spirit allows circumstances that gently demand abandonment to ourselves.

A Prodigal Mother was able to surrender her teenager when she fully submitted and identified with the life and death of The LORD Jesus. Upon this encounter with The LORD, she acknowledged her son was His son.

In your relationships with one another, have the same mindset as Christ Jesus: Who, being in very nature God, did not consider equality with God something to be used to his own advantage; rather, he made himself nothing by taking the very nature of a servant, being made in human likeness.
And being found in appearance as a man, he humbled himself by becoming obedient to death – even death on a cross!
Philippians 2:5-8

I am crucified with Christ: nevertheless I live; yet not I, but Christ liveth in me: and the life which I now live in the flesh I live by the faith of the Son of God, who loved me, and gave himself for me.
Galatians 2:20 (KJV)

Your will be done on earth as it is in heaven.
Matthew 6:10

My Father, if it is possible, may this cup be taken from me. Yet not as I will, but as you will.
Matthew 26:39

Submit yourselves, then, to God. Resist the devil, and he will flee from you.
James 4:7

Since, then, you have been raised with Christ, set your hearts on things above, where Christ is seated at the right hand of God. Set your minds on things above, not on earthly things. For you died, and your life is now hidden with Christ in God. When Christ, who is your life, appears, then you will also appear with Him in glory.
Colossians 3:1-4

17

His Life

When will this end, she deliberated, expressing she could not take another day of the lies, the stealing and destruction. Moreover, the Prodigal Mother continually anticipated additional woe. What will he do next was the question ever before her. She had a sense of dread every time her cell rang.

According to Galatians, Christ is living in us. When this Prodigal Mother appropriated His life, she was empowered. She knew she could take another day because it was Christ living through her who could cope with whatever calamity or stress the future brought. Throughout the day, she whispered, "Thank you Lord Jesus. You are my life." Facing numerous challenges, she stood on this verse, believing and praying without ceasing for her Prodigal.

When Christ, who is your life, appears, then you also will appear with Him in glory.
Colossians 3:4

I am the way, the truth, and the life.
John 14:6

I am crucified with Christ: nevertheless, I live; yet not I, but Christ liveth in me: and the life which I now live in the flesh I live by the faith of the Son of God, who loved me, and gave himself for me.
Galatians 2:20 (KJV)

18

Abba, Father, Papa

Three younger children were exemplary, but the oldest was rebellious and at risk for dropping out of high school. The Prodigal was wreaking havoc in the family and a sense of despair permeated heavily throughout the home.

One day, in the *Secret Place,* she reflected on how she loved all her children equally. Three lavished her with hugs and affirmations – the other with disrespect and hostility. She was grateful when she comprehended it is the same with the Father. He loves her as much as he loves the Reverend Billy Graham or any other great servant of The LORD. Jesus earned extravagant, unconditional love for us.

The Spirit you received does not make you slaves, so that you live in fear again; rather, the Spirit you received brought about your adoption to sonship.
And by Him we cry "Abba, Father."
Romans 8:15

Can a mother forget the baby at her breast and have no compassion on the child she has borne? Though she may forget, I will not forget you!
Isaiah 49:15

And I pray that you, being rooted and established in love, may have power, together with all the Lord's holy people, to grasp how wide and long and high and deep is the love of Christ.
Ephesians 3:17-18

19

Were You a Bad Parent?

A Prodigal Mother had only been born again for a couple of years when we met. Her life before Christ was wild and marked by instability when her children were young. She recounted a life of rebellion with drugs and men, lived out fully before her family. Now teenagers, her children stayed in trouble at school and in the neighborhood. She blamed herself.

As she ruminated over the set of bad examples she had been to her children, she wondered if her past had sealed a negative fate for the family. I remembered a terrible parent in the Bible. It is believed Mannaseh, a king over Israel for fifty-five years, ordered the killing of the prophet Isaiah. He did evil most of his life and forced his own sons to walk through fire as a sacrifice to idols.

"Did you make your children walk through fire?", I asked the Prodigal Mother. Of course not!

Through Mannaseh's story we observe a man who habitually committed atrocities for years. Only when he was taken captive by his enemies did he cry out to The LORD. Despite the wicked activities in which Manasseh engaged, The LORD was moved and answered his prayer.

The extreme example of Mannaseh and other verses comforted and reassured this Prodigal Mother that The LORD is our Redeemer and He can redeem any situation in her family's life. The Word encouraged her to continue walking in her new faith.

And when he prayed to Him, the LORD was moved by his entreaty and listened to his plea.
2 Chronicles 33:13

Mercy triumphs over judgment.
James 2:13

Therefore, if anyone is in Christ, the new creation has come: The old has gone, the new is here!
2 Corinthians 5:17

Christ has redeemed us from the curse of the law, being made a curse or us: for it is written, cursed is every one that hangs on a tree.
Galatians 3:13 (King James 2000 Bible)

If we confess our sins, he is faithful and just and will forgive us our sins and purify us from all unrighteousness.
1 John 1:9

I know that my Redeemer lives.
Job 19:25

20

Beauty for Ashes

"At least I know he is safe when he is in rehab or jail," she related. This Prodigal Mother described a sweet brokenness even as her heart was shattered over her circumstance. She continued to share what she learned during the process.

"I've been in Bible studies for years. I read about the *Secret Place* and knew it represented the LORD'S protection and intimacy with Him, but out of desperation, I found the *Secret Place*. It can't be taught and no one can show you how to get there. The Holy Spirit led me."

This Prodigal Mother recounted hours of alone time with The LORD in which His Spirit was so present she could hardly wait to get there and was never ready to leave. She spent time being quiet, reading her Bible, praying in the Spirit and soaking in worship music. As she basked in sweet communion, she realized The LORD gave her beauty for ashes. Although this was not a path she wanted to walk, she would not trade the priceless joy she learned to share with the Holy Spirit.

*He who dwelleth in the secret place of the most High shall
abide under the shadow of the Almighty.*
Psalm 91:1 (King James Version)

*And provide for those who grieve in Zion-to bestow on
them a crown of beauty instead of ashes, the oil of joy
instead of mourning, and a garment of praise instead of a
spirit of despair. They will be called oaks of righteousness, a
planting of the LORD for the display of his splendor.*
Isaiah 61:3

21

The Faith of Christ

We repeatedly read about and discuss our faith. Let us examine these verses which proclaim HIS faith:

Even the righteousness of God which is by faith of Jesus Christ unto all and upon all them that believe.
Romans 3:22 (KJV)

Knowing that a man is not justified by the works of the law, but by the faith of Jesus Christ, even we have believed in Jesus Christ, that we might be justified by the faith of Christ.
Galatians 2:16 (KJV)

I am crucified with Christ; nevertheless I live; yet not I, but Christ liveth in me: and the life which I now live in the flesh I live by the faith of the Son of God, who loved me, and gave Himself for me.
Galatians 2:20 (KJV)

For we walk by faith, not by sight.
2 Corinthians 5:7 (KJV)

Don't dig up in doubt what the Lord planted in faith.
~Elizabeth Elliott

22

No Condemnation

The pastor's wife glowed after her sons led worship and honored her on Mother's Day. She was understandably gratified for their accomplishments and devotion to The LORD as she innocently posed a rhetorical question, "Do you think I've done a good job?"

A Prodigal Mother in the congregation was envious and wounded by the comment. The answer for the pastor's children was of course, you did an excellent job! However, if the question was reversed about her children, the answer would be no, you did a terrible job.

We asked The LORD's perspective on this. The Prodigal Mother needed to deal with several issues, but one thing was for sure – there is no condemnation for those who belong to Jesus. The enemy may accuse and tell you what a terrible Mom you are, but that is not what the Word says. If The LORD doesn't condemn, then do not condemn yourself. Instead, take it to The LORD and ask him to redeem the Prodigal, the family and the entire situation. Ask Him to turn the mess into a message.

Self-condemnation opens a door for the enemy. Satan detests us. When we self-loathe we partner with him. Why cooperate and assist with his duties? Focus on Jesus and His redeeming power to restore your family and bring your Prodigal back to Himself.

There is therefore no condemnation for those who are in Christ Jesus.
Romans 8:1

I will repay you for the years the locusts have eaten – the great locust and the young locust, the other locusts and the locust swarm – my great army that I sent among you.
Joel 2:25

Since, then, you have been raised with Christ, set your hearts on things above, where Christ is, seated at the right hand of God.
Colossians 3:1

The LORD is close to the brokenhearted and saves those who are crushed in spirit.
Psalm 34:18

Love your neighbor as yourself.
Matthew 22:39

23

Reaping and Sowing

Even as a Prodigal is sowing a bad crop, do you know a Prodigal Mother can simultaneously sow a divine crop? Many Prodigal Mothers weep and sorrow over their children in prayer. Consider tears and hours spent in intercession as seeds. The prayers of a Prodigal Mother avail much. What joy and divine fruit await!

Those who sow in tears will reap with songs of joy.
Those who go out weeping, carrying seed to sow, will return
with songs of joy, carrying sheaves with him.
Psalm 126:5-6

Now Isaac sowed in that land and reaped in the same
year a hundredfold. And the LORD blessed him.
Genesis 26:12

The prayer of a righteous person is powerful and effective.
James 5:16

24

Reaping and Sowing

Galatians informs God is not mocked and we reap what we sow. A Prodigal Mom was anxious because her child was sowing a depraved crop and she was terrified by what he would reap. It is true, we do reap what we sow. God's Word is for our instruction, but we should never be tormented by fear. Perfect love casts out fear.

As we prayed, we discerned the Prodigal Mother needed to continue to intercede because the child was indeed sowing a terrible crop. We remembered our Savior ever lives to intercede for us and He is available to walk through a bad harvest with us.

The Cross satisfied God's wrath so let us always view Scripture in the light of His grace and mercy. Fear for her son's safety was the primary issue, so we prayed she would encounter the perfect love of God, which cast out all fear.

Jesus is Lord over the past, present and future. He is the past, present and future. No beginning. No end. Do not fret about the future. He is already there.

Judy Wills Lowder

*There is no fear in love. But perfect love cast out fear,
because fear has to do with punishment.*
1 John 4:18

*The LORD will surely comfort Zion and will look with
compassion on all her ruins; he will make her deserts like
Eden, her wastelands like the garden of the LORD. Joy
and gladness will be found in her, thanksgiving and the
sound of singing.*
Isaiah 51:3

*He determines the number of the stars and calls them each
by name.*
Psalm 147:4

*The promise is for you and your children and for all who
are far off—for all whom the LORD our God will call.*
Acts 2:39

*Though hand join in hand, the wicked shall not be
unpunished: but the seed of the righteous shall be delivered.*
Proverbs 11:21 (KJV)

25

Avail Yourself of Everything

"If only my son would turn to The LORD, his life would be straightened out. There is so much available to him, if only he would ask," a Prodigal Mother said to me.

As we talked, she acknowledged she was not availing herself of all The LORD's resources either. The Prodigal Mother was continually interceding, yet filled with worry, anxiety and fear.

She further realized The LORD was not only working in her son's life, but her life as well. He was using the trial to conform her to His image. This concept empowered her to continue her walk in Christ with renewed hope.

For in this hope we were saved. But hope that is seen is
no hope at all. Who hopes for what he already has? But
if we hope for what we we do not yet have, we wait for it
patiently.
Romans 8:24-25

And we know that in all things God works for the good of
those who love him, who have been called according to his
purpose. For those God foreknew he also predestined to be

Judy Wills Lowder

*conformed to the image of his Son, that he might be the
firstborn among many brothers and sisters.*
Romans 8:28-29

*Now to Him who is able to do immeasurably more than all
we ask or imagine, according to His power that is at work
within us,*
Ephesians 3:20

16

Total Surrender

The gift of mercy hinders my understanding for why The LORD allows evil in the world, although I intellectually assent it all goes back to the garden. Painful situations, however, can have purpose in our lives. Peter contends these may be necessary for our faith to be refined. We may not think trials are necessary, but Peter knew The LORD when he walked the earth so I concur.

Notice in the verse, "a little while". Relative, isn't it? A little while means ten minutes to most of us, but consider David, who waited fifteen years to become King after he was anointed by Samuel.

What about Abraham? Natural time had expired for Sarah to have children, but The LORD allowed them to wait twenty-five years for Isaac. Followers of Jesus waited fifty days for the coming of the Holy Spirit.

Prodigal Mothers experience pain for different periods of "a little while". It often seems interminable, but Peter exhorts the circumstance will purify your faith, more precious than gold, which is perishable. Prodigal Mothers often describe an intense pain equivalent to the heat which takes gold to liquidity. Similarly, our faith is purified and refined.

James, likewise, instructs believers to count our trials as joy so that we may be mature and complete. This trial will result in praise, glory and honor when Jesus Christ is revealed. Don't waste your heart break. Allow the LORD to work in it and through it.

In all this you greatly rejoice, though now for a little while you may have had to suffer grief in all kinds of trials. These have come so that the proven genuineness of your faith—of greater worth than gold, which perishes even though refined by fire—may result in praise, glory and honor when Jesus Christ is revealed.
1 Peter 1:7

Consider it pure joy, my brothers and sisters, when you face trials of many kinds, because you know the testing of your faith produces perseverance.
James 1:3

And we know that in all things God works for the good of those who love him, who have been called according to his purpose. For those God foreknew he also predestined to be conformed to the image of his Son, that he might be the firstborn among many brothers and sisters.
Romans 8:28-29

Now faith is confidence in what we hope for and assurance about what we do not see.
Hebrews 11:1

27

He Will Finish What He Started

An exasperated Prodigal Mother recounted her son was living an ungodly life after being infant dedicated and raised in the church. He loved the youth group and the family was there every time the doors opened. The pastor preached grace so she was perplexed at the rebellious lifestyle.

We revisited the infant dedication. The Prodigal Mother and her husband fulfilled their commitment to raise the child up in The LORD. She was now constrained to surrender him to The LORD. Hence, the Prodigal was dedicated as an infant and surrendered as an adult.

Shabar struggled with this concept and with the guidance of the Holy Spirit, we hopefully persevere. This Prodigal Mother was fortified with the spiritual understanding The LORD was going to finish the good work which He began in her son and family.

Being confident of this, that He who began a good work in you will carry it on to completion until the day of Christ Jesus.
Philippians 1:6

Judy Wills Lowder

For it is God who is at work in you, both to will and to act
for His good purpose.
Philippians 2:13

But when He, the Spirit of truth, comes, He will guide you
into all the truth.
John 16:13

We continually ask God to fill you with the knowledge of
his will through all the wisdom and understanding that
the Spirit gives.
Colossians 1:9

28

Total Surrender

She described the impact her son's enmity had on the family and feared she was on an emotional brink. It was scary because this Prodigal Mother thought she could not continue. She was quizzical when I affirmed she probably could not take it anymore, but there was something much better than trying to continue on in her own strength. No, she was not on the brink of an emotional breakdown. This Prodigal Mother was on the precipice of experiencing power, love and a sound mind.

But he said to me, "My grace is sufficient for you, for my power is made perfect in weakness." Therefore, I will boast all the more gladly about my weaknesses, so that Christ's power may rest on me. That is why, for Christ's sake, I delight in weaknesses, in insults, in hardships, in persecutions, in difficulties. For when I am weak, then I am strong.
2 Corinthians 9-10

Judy Wills Lowder

*I pray that out of His glorious riches He may strengthen
you with power through His Spirit in your inner being.*
Ephesians 3:16

Finally, be strong in the LORD and in His mighty power.
Ephesians 6:10

I can do all this through Him who gives me strength.
Philippians 4:13

The Sovereign LORD is my strength.
Habakkuk 3:19

*The LORD, the LORD himself, is my strength and my
defense; he has become my salvation.*
Isaiah 12:2

*He gives strength to the weary and increases the power of
the weak.*
Isaiah 40:29

*But those who hope in the LORD will renew their strength.
They will soar on wings like eagles; they will run and not
grow weary, they will walk and not be faint.*
Isaiah 40:31

*The LORD is my strength and my shield; my heart trusts
in him, and he helps me. My heart leaps for joy, and with
my song I praise him. The LORD is the strength of His
people, a fortress of salvation for his anointed one.*
Psalm 28:7-8

God is our refuge and strength, an ever-present help in trouble.
Psalm 46:1

For God hath not given us the spirit of fear; but of power, and of love, and of a sound mind.
2 Timothy 1:7 (KJV)

29

Wounds We Cannot See

A family situation adversely affected one out of three children. In fact, a therapist posited the occurrence was the root of the Prodigal's rebellion and addiction.

The Prodigal Mother took on unintended condemnation from the therapist and was consumed with regret. "I would have handled things differently if I had known," she said. Why did he harbor resentment when the others got over it? We agreed it didn't make sense, but if it hurts, it hurts.

I assured the Prodigal Mother her son's behaviors were not her fault. We parent the best we know and she was not to blame. As she cried, I emphasized to her several times, "It is not your fault."

The teen had invisible scars. Many times the child who is the hardest to love needs it the most. Thankfully The LORD has the anecdote for all our wounds, both mental and physical.

But he was pierced for our transgressions, he was crushed for our iniquities; the punishment that brought us peace was on him, and by his wounds we are healed.
Isaiah 53:5

Is there no balm in Gilead? Is there no physician there? Why then is there no healing for the wound of my people?
Jeremiah 8:22

The LORD is close to the brokenhearted and saves those who are crushed in spirit.
Psalm 34:18

Judy Wills Lowder

30

No Weapon Shall Prosper

Unforgiveness is a tormenter and there were so many she needed to forgive. The goal is to forgive as quickly as we want the LORD to forgive us. As we advanced through a forgiveness exercise, she named her ex-husband, herself, her Prodigal child and others.

The most problematic for this Prodigal Mother was forgiveness towards a neighbor who embellished and disseminated information about herself and her child, which was shared in confidence. They raised their children together and the sense of betrayal was intense. "The truth is awful enough," she said, as she faced an impasse, "there was no need to add on." The gossip had recirculated back to her more than once.

Isaiah differentiates between the words spoken against us and the person who spoke the words. We condemn words spoken against us, but we never condemn a person. This Prodigal Mother made a decision of her will to forgive the former friend. As she discovered the LORD'S deep, deep love, her feelings lined up with her decision and bitterness melted away.

*"No weapon that is formed against you will prosper;
And every tongue that accuses you in judgment you will
condemn. This is the heritage of the servants of the LORD,
and their vindication is from Me," declares the LORD.
Isaiah 54:17 (NASB)*

*Get rid of all bitterness, rage and anger, brawling and
slander, along with every form of malice. Be kind and
compassionate to one another, forgiving each other, just as
in Christ God forgave you.
Ephesians 4:31-32*

*Bear with each other and forgive one another if any of you
has a grievance against someone.
Forgive as the LORD forgave you.
Colossians 3:13*

*Even if they sin against you seven times in a day and seven
times come back to you saying "I repent",
you must forgive them."
Luke 17:3-4*

31

The Mother
Not the Potter

"He was supposed to be a Pastor. We knew when he pretended to preach at age three," she started. Now he was partying, disengaged from anything Christian and never visited without his bold girlfriend who enjoyed shocking the family with vulgarity. She interrupted herself when she processed the words about what her son was supposed to be.

We then began to focus on the Word and how she could surrender her son. We agreed to the following over the next several weeks.

• She figuratively sat her son in an "empty chair" to express her disappointment and an assortment of other emotions. At the end of the session she told her son she loved him no matter what and she was letting him off the "potter's wheel". She let her husband and younger children off the wheel as well.

• She wrote a letter of apology for trying to control and released her son to be himself.

• She looked for the gold in the girlfriend and made a list of traits she chose to like. She memorized affirmations she could genuinely speak to the young

woman. These included:
- "You have a great sense of humor and a contagious laugh."
- "Your career is important. I can tell you work hard and deserve success."
- "You are really considerate of my son and always looking out for him."

The Prodigal Mother found relief for herself and as a result, her son chose to visit and spend more time with the family, both with and without his girlfriend.

We are the clay. You are the potter; we are all the work of your hand.
Isaiah 64:8

For we are God's handiwork, created in Christ Jesus to do good works; which God prepared in advance for us to do.
Ephesians 2:10

Being confident of this, that He who began a good work in you will carry it on to completion until the day of Christ Jesus.
Philippians 1:6

For it is God who works in you to will and to act in order to fulfill his good purpose.
Philippians 2:13

Your kingdom come, your will be done, on earth as it is in heaven.
Matthew 6:10

Made in the USA
Middletown, DE
22 March 2018